LETTERS TO MITCHELL

A FATHER'S VOICE FOR THE MAN YOU CAN BECOME

CHRISTIAN A. DICKINSON

Title: *Letters to Mitchell*
Subtitle: *A Father's Voice for the Man You Can Become*
Written by: Christian A. Dickinson

Illustrations by: Learning Engineered LLC
Published by: Learning Engineered Publishing

Library of Congress Control Number:
ISBN (Print Hardback): 978-1-965741-55-9

First Edition: 2026

Printed & Created in: United States of America
Text and Illustration Copyright © 2025

Learning Engineered Publishing is a division of Learning Engineered LLC and a subsidiary of Carpe Diem Unlimited Holdings, Inc.

LEARNING ENGINEERED
PUBLISHING

CONTENTS

DEDICATION

To Mitchell —
These pages are not advice.
They are scars turned into signposts,
regrets forged into a roadmap, prayers
whispered in the dark so you won't have
to learn the hard way.
May you read them slowly,
live them boldly,
and one day pass them on—
not as rules, but as proof that
grace still writes straight with crooked lines.
You were born for more than survival.
You were born to become.
I'm proud to call you son.
Now go be the man God already sees.

— Dad

"I have no greater joy than to hear that my children are walking in the truth."— 3 John 1:4

FOREWORD

BY MORGAN CHAMPION-DICKINSON

As Christian's wife and Mitchell's mother, I've watched this book grow from whispered prayers to the pages you now hold. These words aren't theories. They're battle-tested truths from a man who has stumbled, risen, and chosen grace again and again.

Mitchell, when you're old enough to read these pages, know your dad wrote every line with the deepest love.

And to every reader holding this book—may these letters inspire you to write your own legacy.

— Morgan

EPIGRAPH

Grace writes straight with crooked lines

—live scarred, love fiercely, listen for the Whisper.

PART I — ROOTS

Every legacy begins with roots.

Before you build, achieve, chase, or conquer anything, you must know where you come from and who stands beside you. These two chapters form the foundation of your life—honor and partnership. The world will pressure you to lead loudly; God teaches men to begin quietly, at home, learning love in its truest forms.

Chapter 1

Take Care of Your Mom

"All that I am, or hope to be, I owe to my angel mother."
— Abraham Lincoln

"Honor your father and your mother, so that you may live long in the land the Lord your God is giving you." (Exodus 20:12)

Mitchell, my mother—your grandmother—died before your mom and I married. When she was gone, I realized the emotional safety net I'd always taken for granted had vanished. I can still picture her kitchen that day: coffee, her favorite scent, lingering in an empty house. Time ran out, and I never saw it coming.

Don't make the mistake I made. Honor isn't guaranteed by time; it's forged in the moments you choose.

Jesus understood this deeply. Hanging on the cross—blood draining, lungs failing—He still made sure His mother had someone to care for her (John 19:26–27). Honor isn't a greeting card; it's a lifestyle.

Exodus 20:12 promises that honoring your parents leads to blessing and longevity. Ephesians 6:2–3 echoes this, calling it "the first commandment with a promise." God ties honor to prosperity because family isn't optional—it's foundational.

You'll be tempted to outsource honor. Flowers on Mother's Day. A check when the roof leaks. A polite text. Those are receipts—not relationship.

Your grandma once told me, "I'd rather have your time than your signature." It stung because she was right.

Care looks like:

- **Showing up** when the casserole brigade goes home.

- **Listening carefully**—hearing the difference between "fine" and fine.

- **Serving quietly**—changing the air filter before she asks.

- **Protecting her heart**—from gossip, neglect, and your own sharp tongue.

One day, I will be gone. Your mom will still be here—maybe needing the arm you once needed. Be the son who kneels. She held you when you were helpless; return that tenderness.

Playbook

- Listen twice as much as you talk.

- Serve before you're asked.

- Cover her with prayer.

- Thank her out loud—every time she makes you better.

Reflection Prompt

Write one memory of your mom's care that shaped you. How can you honor her this week?

Scriptural Deep Dive

Read John 19:25–27. Why did Jesus prioritize His mother while dying? Discuss it with a mentor.

CHAPTER 2

FINDING YOUR 'ĒZER

"**Then the Lord God said, 'It is not good that the man should be alone; I will make him a helper fit for him.'**"
— **Genesis 2:18**

Mitchell, the world will tell you a helper is someone who follows behind you. Scripture tells a different story.

The Hebrew word **'ēzer** appears twenty-one times in the Bible. It describes God's rescuing strength—His power to save, defend, and stand with His people. When the psalmist cries, "God is my help ('ēzer)," (Psalm 70:5) he isn't talking about a sidekick. He's talking about a warrior.

So when God said He would make Adam "a helper suitable for him," He wasn't creating a servant. He was giving him a **warrior-companion**, equal and opposite, fierce and faithful—reflecting God's own nature as rescuer.

Somewhere along the way, the Church shrank that word into something small. But heaven never did.

I learned this the hard way in my first marriage, where I confused leadership with hierarchy. With your mom, I learned what partnership actually looks like: a woman who challenges me, prays fiercely, stands firm when I wobble, and calls me upward.

Your 'ēzer—your future wife—is not meant to flatter you. She is meant to **fortify you**.

Pray for her now.
Become the man worthy of her strength.
And when you meet her, thank God for the rescue.

Guest Insight from Mom

"Being an 'ēzer means mutual rescue. Christian's vulnerability let me step in as his warrior, and vice versa. Mitchell, seek someone who fights with you, not for control." — Morgan

Reflection Prompt

List three qualities of an 'ēzer. How are you developing them in yourself?

Scriptural Deep Dive

Study Psalm 33:20 and Genesis 2:18 together. What does God's role as 'ēzer teach you about marriage?

PART II — GRIND

Ambition will test you long before it rewards you. The grind is where men are shaped: in early mornings, late nights, quiet sacrifices, and unseen obedience. This part teaches you how to build a life without losing your soul. Success is good. Character is better. And the Kingdom demands both.

Chapter 3

Chasing #1

"The will to win is not nearly as important as the will to prepare to win." — Bobby Knight

I've stood on podiums with medals around my neck—and sat alone in empty gyms at 5 a.m. while the people I loved slept without me. Winning demands everything. Some of what I gave, I regret.

I missed most of your cousin's games for "one more practice round." The medal gathers dust; the regret remains.

Chase #1, son. But chase it on your knees first.

When Jesus taught the Parable of the Talents (Matthew 25:14–30), He wasn't praising ambition; He was praising *faithful stewardship*. God cares less about the trophy and more about how you pursued it.

Playbook

- Set God-sized goals. Pray over them weekly.

- Protect family time—schedule it like a meeting with God.

- Celebrate small wins—consistency compounds.

Reflection Prompt

What is your current #1 pursuit? Does it align with eternity?

Scriptural Deep Dive

Read Philippians 3:12–14. What does "pressing on" look like in your life?

CHAPTER 4

RELATIONSHIPS OVER RESULTS

"People will forget what you said, people will forget what you did, but people will never forget how you made them feel." — Maya Angelou

"If I have the gift of prophecy and can fathom all mysteries and all knowledge... but do not have love, I am nothing" (1 Corinthians 13:2).

R esults are receipts—proof you showed up. Relationships are roots—proof you stayed.

Jesus didn't build the Kingdom on metrics. He built it around meals, tears, touch, and time. The disciples forgot half His teachings, but they never forgot how He loved them.

I once prioritized a business deal over a friend in crisis. The deal closed; the friendship cracked. I would trade the results for that relationship now.

At every table ask:

Did I make them feel like royalty in the image of God?

Reflection Prompt

Recall a time someone made you feel valued. Replicate it today.

Scriptural Deep Dive

Study 1 Corinthians 13. Choose one attribute of love to practice daily.

CHAPTER 5

MONEY IS A RUSTY TOOL

"Too many people spend money they haven't earned, to buy things they don't want, to impress people they don't like." — Will Rogers

M oney is a tool—useful, but never ultimate. Treat it like a rusty screwdriver: functional, simple, capable of building something good when handled wisely.

Before you buy, ask:

- Does this serve God's Kingdom or my ego?

- Will I remember this purchase in ten years—or the person I shared it with?

- Will this simplify my life or complicate it?

I once chased careers that cost me peace, rest, and family time. The paydays sparkled; the soul rusted.

CHAPTER 6

GARBAGE IN, GARBAGE OUT

"As a man thinketh in his heart, so is he." — Proverbs 23:7

Your mind is a forge, not a landfill.
What you feed it becomes who you are.

Philippians 4:8 is your filter: whatever is true, noble, pure, lovely, admirable—think on these things.

The world is loud. Anger is marketed. Outrage is monetized. The feed is engineered to steal your peace.

Beware the company you keep—
toxic voices erode character slowly, pulling you into shadows that dim your light.

Choose companions who sharpen iron, not rust it.

Guard what your eyes linger on.
Images and stories that corrupt seep into the soul, twisting desires and dulling discernment.
Seek content that builds virtue, not vice.

Silence is strategy.
Truth is nourishment.
Wisdom is armor.

Reset Routine

- Phone facedown.

- Three deep breaths.

- One thing you're grateful for.

- One verse before one reel.

Reflection Prompt

Log your media and influences for one day.
Replace one "garbage" input with Scripture.

Scriptural Deep Dive

Memorize Psalm 119:105.
Let God's Word light your path.

PART III — KINGDOM

You were born into a world of noise, pressure, and competing truths. But the Kingdom of God is simple: obedience, discernment, and faith. These chapters will show you how to see through the fog—how to live with clarity when the world sells confusion. The Kingdom is steady. The King is near. Keep your ears open.

Chapter 7

God Is Not Dead

"God is not dead; He is alive and working miracles in the hearts of those who believe."
— Inspired by Billy Graham

Mitchell, you were born four weeks early—your head fitting in my palm. After one day, your breathing rapidly increased. The doctor said, "We're moving him to NICU." Your mom collapsed in tears. I stared at the clock: exactly 30 hours since your first cry.

I had just finished a commentary on the number 30—
Jesus began His ministry at 30;
Judas betrayed Him for 30 pieces of silver.

In that sterile room, God whispered through a number:
He's in My hands.

Four days later, you came home—lungs strong, eyes wide, a miracle wrapped in a blanket.

That number became a promise to me:
When God counts to thirty, redemption is always the next breath.

Miracles aren't always parted seas.
Sometimes they're parted pride.
Parted fear.
A heart grafted to flesh (Ezekiel 36:26).

Start here:

- Read the red letters.

- Confess the rust.

Ask for one breadcrumb of light.
He's generous with breadcrumbs.

Reflection Prompt

Write down one miracle—large or small—you've experienced.

Scriptural Deep Dive

Read John 20:30–31.
What modern signs strengthen your belief?

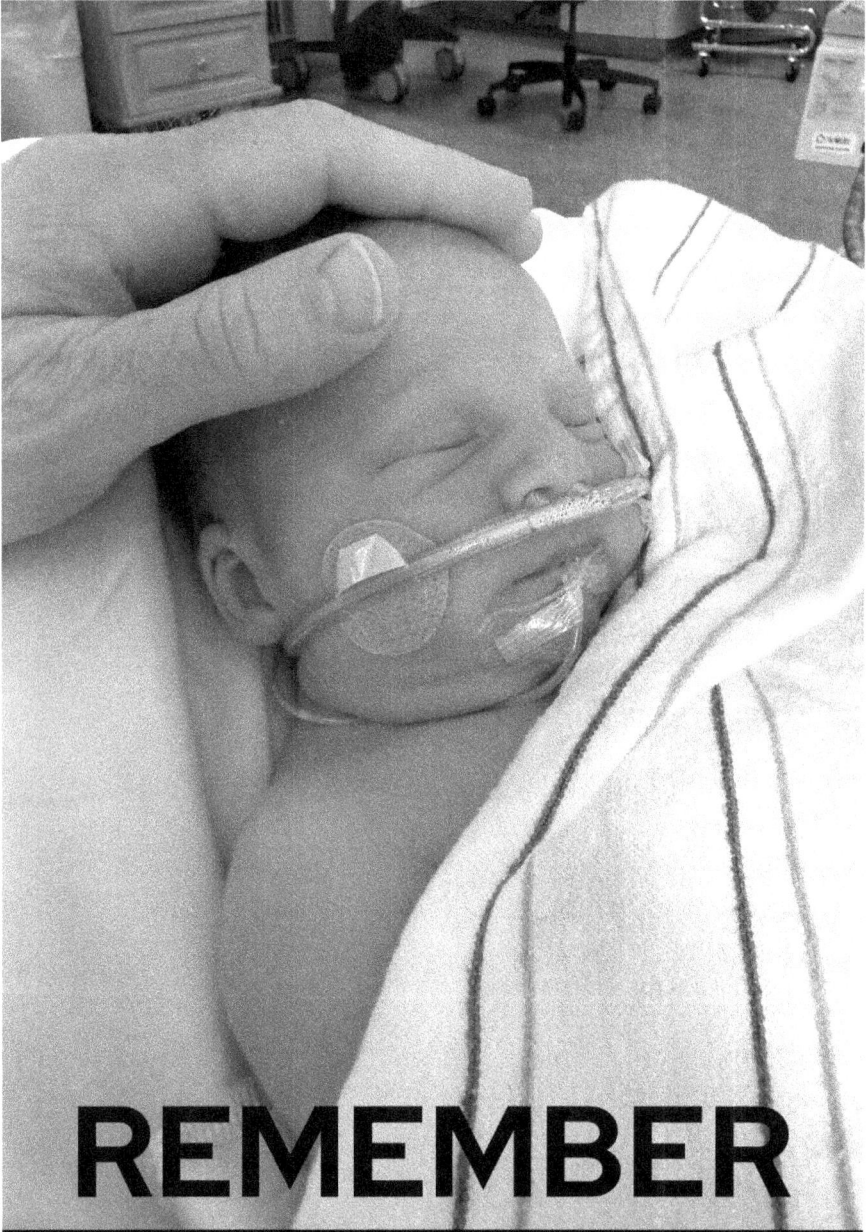

REMEMBER
HOW FRAGILE LIFE IS

Chapter 8

Skip the Möbius Strip

"Politics is the art of looking for trouble... and applying the wrong remedies." — **Groucho Marx**

I keep a postcard of a Möbius strip above my desk—one side, one edge, endless loop. That's politics. Outrage is the engine. Division is the fuel. Every side sells subscriptions to the disease.

Before you rage, ask:

1. Who benefits if I'm angry?

2. What fear is this feeding?

3. Is this Kingdom work—or platform padding?

The Kingdom runs on obedience, not elections. Jesus didn't campaign before Pilate. He spoke truth, then submitted to a cross that conquered what no government could.

Playbook

1. Stay informed, not inflamed.

2. Pray for your leaders—it's harder to hate the man you intercede for.

3. Serve locally. The gospel moves faster neighbor-to-neighbor than bill-to-bill.

4. Post nothing. Mow one widow's lawn this month.

Chapter 9

Follow the Money

"The love of money is the root of all evil." — 1 Timothy 6:10

Satan's oldest trick isn't the blatant lie; it's the half-truth with a receipt. Jesus faced it in the wilderness: "Turn stones to bread"—a "study" with one participant, zero controls, clear agenda.

Train your eyes:

Who paid? Follow the grant, the donor, the dark pool.

Who benefits? If the conclusion sells something, smell rust.

How many? Forty-seven TikTokers ≠ Leviticus.

How blind? Double-blind beats anecdote; peer-reviewed beats press release.

What's missing? Buried data is the sermon.

Keep Proverbs 18:17 folded in your Bible: "The first to speak seems right—until someone examines him."

Truth survives cross-examination.

CHAPTER 10

GET DIRTY

"Whatever you do, work at it with all your heart, as working for the Lord." —Colossians 3:23

J esus didn't save the world from a corner office. He knelt in Gethsemane sweat, washed fishermen's feet, and let Roman mud mix with His blood.

Four dirty truths

Friction forges. Scarred hands build legacies.

Failure fertilizes. Every collapsed roof is compost.

Sweat sanctifies. Labor like the curse is being reversed (Genesis 3:19).

Dirt democratizes. Kings and kids kneel in the same soil.

Ruin the shoes.
Split the jeans.
Let the sun bake the lesson into your skin.

When a suit asks how you built it, show him the scar on your palm from the day the drill slipped.

That's the signature no AI can forge.

CHAPTER 11

BE AN AUTODIDACT

"I have never let my schooling interfere with my education." — Mark Twain

M oses stuttered through Pharaoh's court with forty years of desert tutoring. David wrote psalms between sheep and slingshots. Jesus recruited fishermen, not Pharisees.

I learned to wire a house from YouTube at 2 a.m. while your mom slept. I learned marriage from a revelation the Lord gave me—wrote a book, read it five times, and I'll read it five more. I learned fatherhood in the school of hard knocks—your first weeks were the training ground.

Syllabus no university prints

- Curiosity is tuition.

- Failure is the lab.

- Mentors are textbooks with a pulse.

- Application is the exam.

Never let schooling interfere with education.
The sheep need a shepherd, not a sheepskin.

Chapter 12

Know the Voice of the Lord

"Know the voice of the Lord." — David Victor Dickinson

The Sunday before my dad died, he pulled me aside and said exactly that. I brushed it off—"Yeah, fine, Dad." He died of a heart attack that Wednesday.

Those final words became the only ones that truly matter. Pass that test, and the Kingdom starts here—now.

I'll go one step further:

"Know the voice of the Lord—and follow it." — Christian Alan Dickinson

Every mistake I've made? I didn't listen—or didn't obey.

Thirty-day challenge

1. One red-letter verse (Jesus' words).

2. One obedience.

3. No excuses.

The Spirit of the living God is the tutor.
Ears open wide.

Dad's Last Page

The words I'll keep saying — even if I'm not here to speak them.

Mitchell—

If one day you open this book and I'm not here to finish the sentence, here are the shortcuts I lived by.

- **Carpe Diem**—but pray it into purpose first.

- **Begin with the end**—eternity is the only deadline.

- **Put first things first**—God. Family. Mission.

- **Skate to where the puck is going**—vision beats speed.

- **Fail fast**—scars are tuition.

- **Feedback is gift**—listen like your future depends on it.

- **Love is a verb**—show, speak, stay.

- **Fill their buckets**—yours runs over.

- **This too shall pass**—hold pain loose, hope tight.

- **You miss 100% of the shots you don't take**—courage is fear that prayed.

- **Attitude is everything**—you don't control the storm; you control the sail.

I said these every day I breathed. Now you carry them.

I'm not gone—I'm just ahead on the road.
Keep walking.
I'll meet you at the gate.

— Dad
(P.S. I love you. Louder than thunder. Always.)

About the Author

Christian A. Dickinson is a husband, father, educator, and author whose life's work centers on shaping hearts before headlines. After the end of his first marriage, he found redemption in a second chance with Morgan and their children, Darcy and Mitchell. Through Learning Engineered Publishing, he equips families with resources that build character and faith.

He lives in Florida with his wife, Morgan Champion-Dickinson, where they lead family-run companies devoted to turning scars into signposts—one raw letter at a time.

MORE BY THE AUTHOR

Letters to Darcy: A Father's Voice for the Woman You Can Become — Companion volume.

Roar of 'Ēzer: Reclaiming God's Vision for Women's Strength

Full Circle: Pregame — A Devotional for Athletes